Are You HEALED?
Supernatural Salvation

Arlene A. Luther

"Are You Healed?" Supernatural Salvation

Arlene A. Luther

Copyright © 2016 Arlene Luther
ISBN: 978-0-578-18492-0

All rights reserved. No part of this publication may be reproduced, stored in a retrieval system, or transmitted in any form or by any means—electronic, mechanical, photocopy, or any other—except for brief quotations in printed reviews.

All scripture references are from the King James Version, Public domain.

Contact information for author:
Arlene A. Luther
4541 N. 65th Street
Omaha, NE 68104
arlenealuther@gmail.com

This book is dedicated to you, the reader, wherever you are in your journey upon the Earth.
It is dedicated to wellness.

Table of Contents

FOREWORD..I

INTRODUCTION...III

Part One

Healing Testimony with Supernatural Encounters

CHAPTER ONE..1

Saved

While Yet a Sinner
New York, New York
Jehovah-Jireh, My Destiny
God Cares
God is Spirit
God Communicates Compassion
God's Angels Communicate
God Overlooks Quite a Bit of Failure
God Is an Expert at Turning Weakness into Glory
God Identifies Nefarious Spirits Null and Void
Your Task

CHAPTER TWO..17

Called to Fast

How to Overcome Infirmities According to Bible Fasts
Listen to God: Personal Acknowledgement from Jehovah
Biblical Food Fasts
Fasting from the Marriage Bed
The Infirmity of David and Solomon
Uriah's Fast

CHAPTER THREE...23

Called to Prayer

How to Overcome Infirmities According to Prayer
Apostolic Gifts Stirred Through the Laying on of Hands
Edification Language
Intercessory Prayer: Speaking in Tongues Brings Results

CHAPTER FOUR..29

Overcoming the Spirit of Infirmity

Childhood Silence
A Battle for Life
Ministering Angels: Seeing in Two Dimensions to the Good
Planned Resistance: God's Way to Healing the Physical Body

CHAPTER FIVE...37

Nature's Supplements Checklist

CHAPTER SIX 41

The Impressive Lion of Judah Versus the Destroyer Angel
The "Seer" Anointing

CHAPTER SEVEN 49

The Powerless Python Spirit Versus the Ordinary Woman of Faith

CHAPTER EIGHT 51

Twenty Biblical Healing Declarations

CHAPTER NINE 57

Epiphany: The Happy Wedding Day

CHAPTER TEN 59

Surprise Vision: "Caught Up"

CHAPTER ELEVEN 61

Victory

Ministry on Earth: Seed Healings
Ministry on Earth: Seed Preaching
The Great Commission: Romans Road for Everyone

CHAPTER TWELVE..65
Prosperity Is Answered Prayer

Part Two

How Fallen Angels Work to Hinder God's
Communication to Us on Earth
Nefarious Influences Identified According to the Bible

Nefarious Influences Explained as Infirmities........70

Passive Spirits..71
   Spirit of Fear
   Spirit of Bondage
   Spirit of Heaviness: Observe Negative Energy

Active Spirits Work to Overcome God............................75
   Seducing Spirit
   Perverse Spirit
   Lying Spirit
   Spirit of Confusion
   Harassing Spirits
   Sickness
   Poverty Hinders God's Communication

END NOTES FOR FURTHER READING

Appendix..81

    For Further Reading
    What Do Friends and Colleagues Say?
    Songs
    Contact Information
    "Good News Fast Tract"

Foreword

I trust that God will honor your heart to help others with fruit commensurate to the root of your life.

Pastor Steve Warriner
Former Pastor: Abundant Life Christian Church
Presently Called to Apostolic Ministry

Introduction

And He said unto me, "My grace is sufficient for thee: for my strength is made perfect in weakness"
(2 Corinthians 12: 9)

God is not without understanding. Satan is not without understanding. We are. Just as God intends happiness and wellness for us, the fallen archangel, Lucifer, intends severe harm. In this testimony, the Lord has illustrated through my life's experience and observation, God's good intention toward us does prevail in eternity past, present, and future.

The ability of the Father, Son, and Holy Spirit to connect with our faith in each dispensation of time enables us to overcome the evil intended for us on this Earth, thus creating Heaven on Earth while it proves God's Glory. God's warring angels, dispensed by Jesus' administration from third Heaven are on assignment today. They overcome fallen spirits, also on assignment, that hinder us on command from Lucifer in second Heaven. God's angels guard and protect us through Christ's direction of omnipresence.

This book describes the battle we fight in faith to conquer our infirmities: lack of health and happiness, and how to overcome the influence of second Heaven fallen angels and principalities through faith, persistence, deliverance, and testimony in Christ. God's third Heaven angels still battle for us today, and they help bring us victory. Christ and Lucifer still battle today. It is still God's dominion. He is the same yesterday, today and forever.

After conversion, we are seeking God, precept upon precept, faith upon faith, in proven life experiences that mature us in the knowledge of God. El-Shaddai supplies all our needs in victory. Keep in mind the book of Revelation where it declares victory is that of Christ, no matter how the battle rages in one individual's life, in churches blind to their own sin within, or Armageddon.

Through many years, God's watch, both before and after conversion, for my personal protection, healing, and discernment in living is shown throughout this book. Often I was unaware of the battle here on Earth, and lived merrily along the way. I am in Christ now. I abide with the Holy Spirit in my life. Conversion is not the only experience that gives Glory to God on Earth.

For some reason, God desired for me an awareness of the battle that rages. He convinced me He loves me. I have noticed there are many Christians who do not see the warfare. I hope this book gives the reader eyesight, personal encouragement to "see" and overcome the wiles of the devil in life. I hope it discourages superficial behavior and judgments through gossip. I am thankful to live in Jehovah-Shalom, the peace of God each and every day.

Life is anything but easy for many persons on this Earth. There is almost always more to a person's life than you can see or understand apart from the Divine intention of God, our Father. This book is my ministry gift to you, the reader.

Arlene A. Luther (maiden name Caudill)

Part One

Healing Testimony
with
Supernatural Encounters

Saved

CHAPTER ONE

"But God commendeth His love for us, in that, while we were yet sinners, Christ died for us" (Romans 5:8)

While Yet a Sinner

While I was in college in the 60s, I slipped out of the dorm after the 9:00 P.M. curfew. I was walking at night quite a distance to my boyfriend's apartment all alone. Just off campus, I heard an athletic person approaching rapidly behind me, walking much faster than I could. My first impulse was to run, but I refrained, knowing I would be easily overtaken. It is amazing to me how the Holy Spirit watched over me in that situation even though my initial reaction was flight. I was not born again, but I was sensitive to God's leading. There was no time to question.

A lighted intersection was before me to my left. I was guided by the Lord and my guardian angel to stand directly under this light in the middle of the intersection rather than break into a run. I obeyed. My Mom and Dad were strict as I grew up. We did not question them. As I turned toward the attacker under this street light, he turned to the dark. I noticed a knife exposed in his hand as he went off to find another victim. In an instant, I was saved that night. "But God commendeth His love for us, in that, while we were yet sinners, Christ died for us" (Romans 5:8).

Thanks to the wisdom of God that dark night, I made my parents happy when they attended my college graduation a year or so after that. I do not remember ever sharing this night with them. I was the first in my family to graduate from college. It was important to them. Neither of my parents graduated from high school. Graduation had very little meaning to me other than that. My mother, although gifted, went to work after eighth grade. My father worked in Grand Island, Nebraska, after he served as a drill sergeant in the United States Army. His oldest brother stayed to inherit the family farm. The rest of his family had to make new lives for themselves in town. I think now my parents were right, a college education did benefit me and my future children.

New York, New York

New York broadened my perspective of life in vast ways. Out in the evening for a stroll, or on my way to work in early morning, I found the underworld of New York City to be shocking. For example, I had never seen or even heard about homosexuals until I saw them in drag along the evening streets of Greenwich Village downtown area. I saw homeless people on my way to work in the morning. I saw a dead man on the street. I saw empty buildings where homeless people found shelter. I began to see dark realities of life. I became aware of more than peaceful fields of wheat or corn in Nebraska. My spirit was still inactive, but I was soon to be experiencing the marvelous contrast found in God's Kingdom on Earth.

For two years, I had the privilege to work at B. Altman and Company on Fifth Avenue. There I enjoyed a peaceful environment in the ladies department (peace that was not found on the subway just outside the building). I enjoyed the basement thrift shop for employees during lunch time and after work when it was open. I was reminded of home as I passed by the Norman Vincent Peale Church for positive thinkers.

There is sharp contrast between darkness and light in New York. Even a naïve young woman from Nebraska had to notice this. There are very poor people here in America. It was real. It bothered me.

With only that thought on my mind, perhaps I could have lasted a while longer in New York. However, another shock to my way of thinking was soon to follow. As I arrived home from work, I heard a commotion in the apartment. I opened the door. I saw a small woman wearing my young husband's shirt to cover her otherwise naked body. He was missing a shirt, but managed to nearly get his pants on before I entered the room. I had a mild breakdown and went home to divorce him. My family did not care for infidelity. I had no children from this marriage.

Jehovah-Jireh, My Destiny

Three years later, I became aware of my Savior, Adonai, when I became spiritually alive. It was a predestined moment determined from eternity past. Saved by the sovereign hand of God in 1972, just after I had entered the bonds of marriage for the second time, my spirit was awakened by the Holy Spirit. It happened shortly after I married Tom R. Luther. God saved me. In His omnipresence mighty God came to me while I was lying in bed. It took this act of God to change my direction from how in the world did I get here to God cares more than I thought. He is so amazing. Before this moment, I had no direction in my life at all.

Contradictory as it may seem, even as a child I talked to God. I was aware of God. I sought God when my favorite cousin was killed in a car accident. This evening was different. I was about to get some inner direction through inner connection. No one needed a personal touch from God more than I did. Something happened. As Bill Gaither said, "He touched me, and now I am whole." What happened to me in bed? I was a different person from one moment before this happened. God loves persons that are not famous or talented. He loves poor and injured persons. He seeks persons without clear direction. He had something to say: It is God whose ways are higher than our ways (Isaiah 55:9). His love is a higher love; it is not based on the thrill of the moment. I was not really a bad person. What was different now? I had acquired motivation I had not previously known about. I was awakened by the Holy Spirit. Honestly, I sometimes wish God had just left me a free spirit without a conscience.

Immediately, the Holy Spirit began to teach His ways. Within a day or so, I received the Billy Graham New Testament my mother was impressed upon by God to send to me at that exact time. I had not considered God deeply before this, although I had gone to church all of my life. I moved along with the flow of life as Tom Luther did. By the way, I understand he is saved today, and moving along with the flow in Christ.

I love Peter for example. He moved along as a fisherman. His idea of fishing was expanded through his friendship with Christ. Consider Nicodemus, in John chapter three. He was a smart, savvy religious leader. He moved along in the flow of things at church. Yet one day he asked Jesus what he needed to do to be saved? What went wrong with Nicodemus? What about Paul? He moved along the religious zealot flow line. He was still a religious zealot after God blinded him to give him time to think. He was still brilliant. That part of Paul did not change. God decided to change his direction in life. After all, he really did need to stop his destructive ways. Saul, we know him as Paul, needed to get healed. He became a famous lover of the faith. Even Peter mistrusted Paul. Most Christians were afraid of him. Yet God saved him one day.

That is what happened to me that day in bed. The next day I became more aware of light and dark as I read and studied my Billy Graham New Testament with motivation to know what had happened to me! There is no reasonable explanation. God does what He wants. When He wants something, there is no changing His mind about it. I know that because I have prayed not my will but Thy will be done in my life way too many times. He has made me strong and resilient rather than weak. God may motivate you. God may expand your knowledge. God may change your direction. God may heal you! I hope you profit from what has happened to me as you continue to read my pilgrim journey to awakening through healing and deliverance.

Keep in mind, God considers me. He honors me. He considers you. He honors you.

He captured my attention as I fell into deep remorse. I had been divorced already. What was to happen now? I had married another almost "perfect" stranger for the second time around, a man I had met three months prior. What can I say? We were destined to give it our best. Our family made it. We all made it after forty years of perseverance in a difficult world.

I accept God as God. It was the Holy Spirit that moved into action and initiated my Bible study. I became what Tom Luther called a Bible thumper. Quite honestly, it is still the best book I have ever read. This is why there is faith, hope and love abide. This is why the greatest of these three is God's love (1 Corinthians 13). Love does not have a quitting time.

God Cares

This was my new life in the Spirit (John 3:5) and in Truth. It was a new beginning. It was good to be alive! I was getting washed in the Word of God every day. In just a few years, three children were born alive to us.

Once I began reading the Bible, I could not stop. In these pages I found comfort. Jesus became my friend. I hope you understand. The Word of God was soon written on my heart and in my mind. I soaked in the Word of God daily, especially the New Testament. I even studied theology. I read a lot of books. This marriage produced three healthy children in God's mercy as I read. Therein I still abide after more than forty years of faith. God is good. I am thankful. This is the way things are in the Kingdom of God on Earth.

God is Spirit

God has expressed Himself to man, through man, in the inspired Word of God, the Bible, profitable for instruction to all ages. He has expressed Himself through the life of Jesus Christ as He lived a spiritual life, second to none. Jesus alone fulfilled the spiritual law literally in His flesh. Neither you nor your wife did. Adam and Eve did not. No religious single person like me, before or since Jesus, ever did either.

The Word became flesh... (John 1:14). Christ's dispensation of time on Earth succeeded, where Adam and Eve had previously failed. No other man is commissioned ever to do what Jesus did again, since He alone gained victory over the fallen angels and their leader Lucifer. That is why the chains of unseen nefarious spiritual influences can be broken off. Adam and Eve lost this battle. So did all of us alive today if it were not for Christ who conquered all. Sometimes we lose this battle unnecessarily and have to fall upon Jesus for victory, the second Adam, who did win the lonely battle at the cross of Calvary. Fallen angels are completely subject to the authority of Jesus Christ. They have no lawful dominion over any Christian for that reason.

Christ's life is now expressed through the Holy Spirit

on Earth. Jesus gave His blood for everyone to overcome covetousness, and other flaws usually from generational spirits over a family, including every type of willful or unwitting sin in man due to undiscerned nefarious influences still at work in the world today. This is why God must see us through Jesus' life. We are protected through Jesus' blood and clear awareness we cannot save ourselves. We are assured of eternal life in the third Heaven, through faith in this historic memory of Jesus' life on Earth. The Holy Spirit unites our Spirit to the Father. He is our faithful companion on Earth. He is our source of dignity and hope alive throughout the world today. Amen.

While I was under the power during my tenure at Institute of Ministry in Minnesota, the Holy Spirit said to me, *"Never forget what Jesus did for you."* I said, "How could I?"

God Communicates Compassion

As you have seen, my destiny was decided by God even when I was not aware of it. I am a good example of God's compassion. God determined His will for me was uncovering both the causes of infirmity for my understanding, and maintaining my dignity as a human being along the way. Christ tells us in 2 Corinthians 12:9 His strength is made perfect in weakness. Overcoming weaknesses through different levels of faith and obedience made me good as seen by Jehovah-Tsid Kenou. I am seen through Christ, my Righteousness. Praise the Lord.

God wishes that no man should perish. God allows

each of us to evolve spontaneously through inquisition and discovery as Dewy, an educator described it. Inquiry: we call it faith, is upward stair steps, or levels of discovery within us toward our Creator and fellow man. Somehow God is able to perfect our destiny by reconciliation to the Creator and planet Earth. It is almost a scientific principle.

After reading about John Dewy in college, and later reading the Bible, I feel like this idea is agreed upon. The Bible says seek and you will find. Knock and the door will be opened to you. This is how it was for me. We as humans, have a desire to work, achieve, and contribute. We love and like to be loved in return. We are like God in that way. He first loved us (Romans 5:8). We seek, question, and discover God's love is unconditional. He is.

God's Angels Communicate

There are two good angels to every one fallen angel (Revelation 12: 4, 9). One third of God's created angels fell with Lucifer. Hell is actually for them—not mankind. Two thirds remained to serve God faithfully forever.

Jesus Christ has dominion over all angelic realms. Christ dispenses angels according to the will of the Father on our behalf. He is the one worthy of this authority. There are nine orders of heavenly angels working for God. These are archangels such as Michael and Gabriel, guardian angels or ministering spirits, virtues, powers, healing, principalities over territories, dominions, thrones, cherubim and seraphim near God's throne, each with six wings (Isaiah 6). Satan has ranks of fallen angels. As you will see in this testimony, they war in vain under the supreme authority of Jesus Christ. We simply acknowledge we have fallen short.

Angels teach. They announce important events like Gabriel did at the birth of Christ. They warn us. They give messages such as mercy or comfort. They judge. They transport us to Heaven when we die. Sometimes our guardian angels transport us in visions before we die. Old and New Testament prophets: for example Ezekiel, Daniel, Apostle Peter, Apostle John, etc. had visions when the Heavens opened. Remember the New Testament vision of John the Apostle called the Apocalypse? It is the most extensive vision anyone has ever had. It is recorded for us in the book of Revelation. John was most likely transported by angels. Revelation is twenty-two chapters in length. What an amazing vision. Melchizedek disappeared to Heaven. Jesus ascended to Heaven after the order of Melchizedek (Hebrews 6:20). They were transported by angels.

Our angels are not resting in Heaven. They are working on our behalf and praising God in Heaven and on Earth. They can move from third Heaven through second Heaven, through the firmament above the Earth to Earth. Sometimes they travel with Jesus when the Heavens open. This is an epiphany. They seem to ascend and descend in a spiritual ladder like Jacob's ladder. Guardian angels protect and fight for us. They influence our thoughts just as fallen angels do. God's angels battle against the fallen angels and their influences. We are told in 1 Corinthians 2:14, things of the Spirit are spiritually discerned. We see what God enables us to see.

God Overlooks Quite a Bit of Failure

I have been notoriously weak in my body most of my life due to penicillin side effects. I could rarely, if ever, pull an A in physical education. P.E. was mandatory when I went to school. In college, one of the women in my swimming class quietly swam the final test for me. I had to let her do this if I wanted to pass the class. An unusual kind of fortitude is what I had in school. That is why I pray. God enables me to pray. Anyone who prays can overcome infirmity. He is the lifter of my soul and spirit, and the healer of my body.

I was always behind the smartest students in my class, even in High School. I noticed this, and they noticed. I took home a lot of books every night. Others did not. I sat at the kitchen table every night after dishes were done and did my homework until I went to bed, while the smart kids were cruising South Locust. My Dad would take us for a root beer float every once in a while to make up for it. I always thought it was kind of him, although we both knew it wasn't the same thing. Little did anyone at home or in school suspicion penicillin side effects keeping me from being super smart. I just kept going. I was busy being me. I was thankful to be on the honor roll. I was well above average as far as I could see. Mother, a gifted woman, told me I was above average; and I believed her. My faith grew as I believed all things are possible to those who believe (Matthew 19:26).

Did I have weaknesses? Consider my ability to overcome another adversity I faced in school due to penicillin in the following example. I did not take chemistry. I cheated in algebra. I had to. The teacher knew it. He left the room. I nervously pulled out my cheat sheet. Everyone heard the paper rustle in the "you could hear a pin drop" room. Quickly I copied and returned the cheat sheet to its hiding place. I somehow got a B or a C on that test. My case to summarize how the Lord communicates His ability to overcome weakness rests. Let God turn it all into His glory.

God Is an Expert at Turning Weakness into Glory

I notice often a saint sees both heavenly and underworld visions in his or her training for life or ministry. I notice the Holy Spirit is there to make sure it goes right if ever we open our mouths in the name of Jesus as a complete novice in front of a church. I never will forget the time I blasted the church prophetically with the Lords' prayer (Matthew 6). That certainly was Heaven on Earth coming from a woman who did not even speak as a child. Similar to Daniel, I was mute: then I had something to say. Amazing! I remember God then moved on my pastor to blast Heaven on Earth is compassion.

Later, I never will get over the time the Holy Spirit took John 3:16 right out of my mouth and floated it in a powerful way to the persons listening. I saw this happen. I am encouraged because my pastor told me, "That is what the Holy Spirit does." I am still amazed every time I think about that. I actually saw the "dove" minister! One woman brought her pencil and paper to me after the service. I asked her to read John 3:16 and the book of Romans. Oh how I love the Pentecostal church's healing ministry through the Holy Spirit on Earth today.

God Identifies Nefarious Spirits Null and Void

What are the scales that hinder us? Most everything that hinders falls under what the Bible calls evil spirits. Evil spirits is an old expression. However, this does describe what the real battle is. It really is not your neighbor. Christ told us to love our neighbor and battle the fallen spirits. We now refer to evil spirits as nefarious influences. At least that is what Dr. Phil says they are. I love his sophisticated terminology.

The main nefarious spirits in the Bible are fear, deaf and dumb, bondage, lying, perverse, lethargy, heaviness, jealousy, haughty, and last but not least, infirmity. Their purpose is to hinder mankind from happiness. Go to Part Two for a description of these spirits as God has enlightened me about them. You can also learn more about Nephilim history in the book of Enoch. You may also be interested in Nephilim Agenda by Randy DeMain. Nephilim were evil fallen angels that intermarried with human women. They created a race of evil giants like Goliath. This was the reason for Noah's flood. Today many ministers talk about other wicked spirits such as the Jezebel spirit. Jezebel spirit is still one of these basic spirits, though. Suffice it to say the story of Jezebel is an excellent illustration of the spirit of jealousy and haughtiness. Jealously includes anger and even murder. Jezebel actually internalized the spirit. It overcame her in the unhappy ending (1 Kings and 2 Kings). Wouldn't you rather be healed?

We in the church hope to avoid spirits overcoming us as we battle just as Elijah did. We have to rely on God's power. Let the evil deeds be bound: Jezebel lost her head and was eaten by dogs. Spare me that. Praise God! We battle for our lives in prayer. Jesus battles with us. We are never alone. I could have done without muteness due to penicillin, a broken back and neck, or nearly getting sucked into a black hole. But I could not let anything stop me. I had to get over it. You will soon hear about it all in this glorious praise testimony and thanksgiving to omnipotent God.

Some persons from the subversive culture seek God. God seeks the subversive culture. It is a spontaneous emergence to God that originates from man's inquisition. The Bible says seek and you will find, or knock and the door will be opened to you. I wrote a paper where I describe this in the title as Man's Search for Meaning. The subversive culture needs God although it is still a great never ending commission on the backs of society to enlighten such.

Many persons may not have the ability to perceive God as always good, or Christ's victory at Calvary is 100% complete. The influence of fallen angels is null and void in our lives even though we must live out parts of it in this dispensation of time to prove the story. Keep in mind, "There is therefore now no condemnation to them which are in Christ Jesus, who walk not after the flesh, but after the Spirit" (Romans 8:1). Please notice the victory you can clearly see in each and every episode of my healing testimony. Honestly, it takes a sage to believe it. It takes a sage to live it!

Keep in mind; everyone has the ability to appreciate a new well in the village. Any person can appreciate a job to earn their own groceries. Third world countries can appreciate a surgeon. The Holy Spirit is present in all of this. He is omnipresent. He can overcome the ignorance of the masses. He can bring the freedom they are striving for as they seek. He can heal the wounded. The healing presence of the Holy Spirit is free if you can tap into it. It is a tangible presence. It can be seen. It can be felt at all levels of society.

Christianity is not a once in a lifetime epiphany: I was born again and that is the end of the story to many persons. To me, it is the beginning of the story! How many times have I been saved? Many! Following is my story as I continue in the present, past, and future omniscient knowledge of God in my life. Just as there are black holes of negative energy, there are also streams of positive energy from third Heaven to Earth. There are both positives and negatives in science. There are both positives and negatives in most anything. Why should the spirit world, the Bible or life be any different? I do not know your preference. I would much rather be caught up in positive eternity well aware of the negative under foot.

My Mom always had confidence I would find a way to make a better world. I guess I did. Although not a prolific person, I was determined to contribute something to the complicated world I found myself living in. Following is a poem she asked me to memorize. It has stayed with me all of these years.

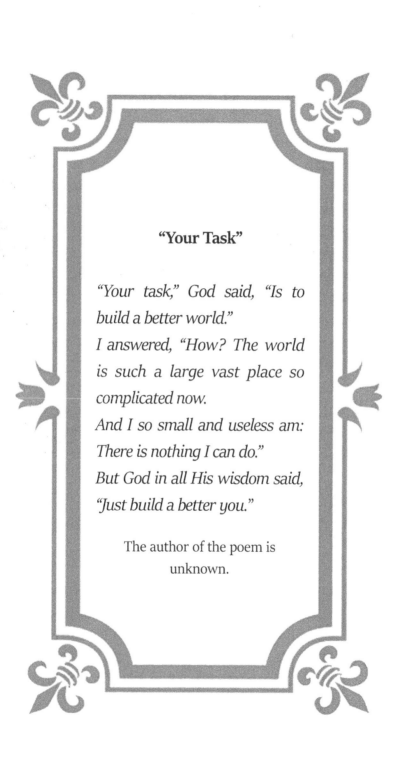

"Your Task"

"Your task," God said, "Is to build a better world."
I answered, "How? The world is such a large vast place so complicated now.
And I so small and useless am: There is nothing I can do."
But God in all His wisdom said, "Just build a better you."

The author of the poem is unknown.

Called to Fast

CHAPTER TWO

"....not as I will, but as thou wilt"
(Matthew 26:39b).

How to Overcome Infirmities According to Bible Fasts

The Lord led me to fast from the beginning. There are many kinds of fasts just as there are many kinds of infirmities. Fasting from food is the most noted type of fast. In the early days I fasted three days and three nights regularly as the Lord instructed me. Recently, the Lord has led me in two twenty-one day fasts. The first was while I attended the Institute of Ministry. I had no food on this fast. I had beverages every other day. This is pretty close to Daniel's fast. He fasted three weeks. He had no wine. He had water. "I ate no pleasant bread, neither come flesh nor wine in my mouth, neither did I anoint myself at all, till three whole weeks were fulfilled" (Daniel 10:3).

The second twenty-one day fast seemed impossible to me. I said to the Lord, "It is more difficult to fast now than when I was a young woman." The Lord did not discuss it further. I am under the impression He is in disagreement with me on this "old age" mentality. I have learned you can tell the Lord anything you want, but if He disagrees, you will ultimately have to give in to His will for your life—that is, if you love Him. He allowed me one small meal each day on the second twenty-one day fast and beverage daily. I was hungry all of the time from when I arose in the morning until I went to bed at night.

I always pray, *"...not as I will but as Thou wilt."* (Matthew 26:39). Jesus prayed that prayer.

Jesus always acknowledged and thanked His Father in everything He asked.

Listen to God:
Personal Acknowledgement from Jehovah

God has a purpose for everything He does. I remember after one food fast, the Lord simply acknowledged me. It was a heart thing. He acknowledged His love presence is sure. That makes this a love story.

It was not the throne of God I had ever reached in sight or flight after that tiresome fast or any other fast, or even praying in tongues with all my might. I was really tired for some reason. I could not be sure if any of it mattered that much. Look how much God gave Daniel after a twenty-one day fast. We still talk about it today. I may have felt as if I had not been able to reach the mountain top. It almost seemed as if I had fallen behind the others I had prayed for. At least I reached the ears of God. At least God acknowledged me.

One thing I have always enjoyed when listening to Billy

Graham is how he is able to tell the old, old story in a new way over and over again. It touched my heart that God acted as he did that day. I acknowledged Him through obedience to many fasts over many years. I think it is knowing my Father still loves me. That knowledge may have been all I needed that day. I needed encouragement. I haven't fasted or prayed in the Spirit much since then. I pray God will enable me again so I can continue in the ministry. This is the old story. God loves us: yesterday, today and forever. He is not whimsical. He is consistent.

Biblical Food Fasts

Some specific Bible references to fast include Luke 4:2, Jesus' forty day fast, Daniel 10:3, Daniels' twenty-one day fast, and Esther 4:16, a corporate fast. These are all fasts from food. Other Bible fasts are not necessarily referred to as fasts. You kind of have to look for them or let the Lord point them out to you.

Fasting from the Marriage Bed

For example, there is such a thing as fasting from the marriage bed. I want to talk about this briefly because I see quite a lot of pride, and at times, even a haughty spirit in couples concerning their marriage beds. Rather than expressing humility before God in a fast from the conjugal relations, most married couples are not aware that this is an option in their devotion to the Lord. Many are oblivious to this expectation, but they think they are holy! They tend to point out how they got lucky and boast loudly about it. I have yet to see a whisperer when it concerns their satisfaction in bed.

I have met a few who do fast from their marriage bed. May I point out to you dear reader, God reasons it is sometimes helpful in your relationship, to use discipline. God is the Holy One. Why? He is a Spirit and does not have orgasms like we animals do. Humans are like the animals in their need for water, food, sleep, air, and orgasm to live. Yes. I said orgasm, not sex.

The purpose for the married couple is not the sex act itself, but climax. There are many sex acts that mean nothing to anyone. Anything from rape to the husband who does not satisfy his wife are "sex acts." Political sex acts happen every day. Sex crimes are abuse. Not any of that is healthy. Marriage is for love and procreation, that is, the next generation. I do not see a reason to argue unless you think we do not need another generation to follow behind us.

What is my point? Could you married folk consider a fast from your marriage bed now and then? The last time I looked, that is totally scriptural. Put your stones down. Single persons and the less fortunate do not need death by stoning because their sex lives are less than perfect. They do not need your sex life flaunted in their face either. Honestly, I am happy for you.

Let's move on with another political look see. Extra-marital sex is a tool many married couples use without any disapproval from anyone socially, both in and out of churches today as well as Bible days. Did you know it is nefarious? Did you ever stop long enough to think you may be harming other persons with this sin as you climb the social ladder of success? David and Solomon are classic examples.

The Infirmity of David and Solomon

David needed sackcloth and prayer after he got caught committing adultery and murder. Why did he need eight wives and concubines to begin with? I do not think the man needed eight wives. He had to overcome the spirit of lethargy and the infirmity of lust. I do not have to point out lust infirmity is accepted in all shapes and forms in society today, including the church.

David and his son, Solomon, are kind of like the economic Bull Run Markets we have in our society today. David crashed. David was disciplined by God for what he did. I am not sure if Solomon ever did crash. Solomon's one thousand wives and concubines I find to be one of the greatest examples of lust infirmity in the Bible. It is comparable to Jezebel except the primary infirmity in Jezebel was jealousy. We know Jezebel did not repent. She loved her infirmity. Did Solomon? We do not know if Solomon repented.

Attitude may save you. Just as Peter wept bitter tears of remorse, David did. Jezebel and Judas did not repent. Yesterday and today we have bulls like Solomon. Many bulls have many wives still today. I wonder if any man on Earth today has one thousand. Some are still with the wives of their youth, the pride of life. We honor the outcome as they honor their wives in repentance.

Uriah's Fast

Let us remember to honor Uriah for a moment as well. I have never heard anyone preach on the obedience of Uriah. I have never heard anyone preach on the faithfulness of Uriah. What? His life does not count in the shadow of David's disobedience and repentance? Why? To God it certainly mattered! It is recorded in the Bible for some reason. I am glad I am here to thank God for the fast of Uriah. Keep in mind, Uriah would not have sex with his wife to honor the king and God during battle. I am here to honor the memory of Uriah. I am here to point out many more of us need to honor God the way Uriah did.

There are other fasts. There is a fast from material comforts. I have been there. It is not a bit of fun to live in lack of anything, especially enough money. The gap between poor and rich in this country is becoming wide. We can fast and provide to others as much as we are able. There are numerous unmentioned fasts in the Bible. There is a fast from people. Praise God! Jesus "withdrew Himself to pray" (Luke 5:16). Everyone needs solitude sometimes. If you have been through a tough experience in life or know a challenge is ahead of you, rest yourself alone from other people to seek God. Paul needed time to recover after being stoned several times by ignorant persons in his life. Fasts heal us. Fasts honor God.

Called to Prayer

CHAPTER THREE

"After this manner therefore pray ye: Our Father which art in heaven, hallowed be Thy name. Thy kingdom come. Thy will be done in earth, as it is in heaven. Give us this day our daily bread. And forgive us our debts, as we forgive our debtors. And lead us not into temptation, but deliver us from evil: For thine is the kingdom, and the power, and the glory, forever. Amen" (Matthew 6:9-13).

How to Overcome Infirmities According to Prayer

I prayed continually from the beginning. It was a burden of prayer. By this I mean it was with me continuously twenty-four seven.

The Acts chapter in my life developed in stages of prayer. I was introduced to the Pentecostal Church right after salvation in July of 1972. A husband and his wife and their small group prayed for quite a while until finally the word Abba came forth from my mouth. "For ye have not received the spirit of bondage again to fear; but ye have received the Spirit of adoption, whereby we cry, Abba, Father" (Romans 8:15). She then clearly spoke in the Hebrew tongue and he interpreted, telling us what God planned to do in the small community where we all lived. It was a profound example of tongues and interpretation of tongues. I never saw them again.

Nothing further happened in the development of Acts 2:3 until the early 1980's when I asked the Lord if He wanted the Pentecostal prayer life called speaking in tongues for my life. I wanted to grow in the Lord. I read and studied the Bible. I asked the Lord about the unusual prayer language. Was it even in accord with Scripture? I had studied the denominational view: this gift was only for those in the dispensation of time following Christ's ascension; the time when the apostles lived and ministered like Christ; this gift was not for our age. I read in the Bible: the Lord gives gifts as He wills. "Seek and ye shall find. Ask and it shall be given you; knock, and it shall be opened to you: For everyone that asketh receiveth; and he that seeketh findeth; and to him that knocketh it shall be opened" (Matthew 7: 7, 8). I prayed: Is this what you desire for me?

Apostolic Gifts Stirred Through the Laying on of Hands

As it turns out, God did want a life of prayer for me beyond what I knew at that point in my walk with Christ. The apostolic gifts God placed in my spirit the moment I was "born again" needed to be activated. I traveled to an apostolic conference where a young minister was preaching. I was called out by the Lord and the apostolic gifts were further awakened by the laying on of hands. The Lord had now moved me from the denominational into the pentecostal and charismatic church theology through the experience of the laying on of hands (Acts 19:6). Soon after this the Lord began to move me into dimensions of prayer.

Edification Language

I continued to ask the Lord, "Do you want this for me?" The edification prayer language began to come forth. I believe this is all the prayer language many Charismatic Christians ever experience because this is all they ever need. As He searched me, He deepened my prayer life. I wrote out a journal of forgiveness. I prayed the levels of prayer in intercession for my children many years which is called speaking in tongues in the pentecostal and charismatic church. The Lord began to move us out of the denominational church into the pentecostal life at this time. The denominational churches, as a rule, do not believe in tongues for this dispensation of the church age. I believe the Lord was leading us into supernatural salvation, supernatural healing and success through the deeper levels of intercessory prayer. I was on the move.

Intercessory Prayer: Speaking in Tongues Brings Results

I had a burden for my children as a single parent (Acts 16:31). I believe their parent father did also. I know their Father, Jehovah-Rohi, did. The professional level of my grown children's success is primarily due to the deep intercessory levels of prayer, hours of speaking in tongues, connecting in faith asking God to shepherd them. We sometimes call it wailing in the church. Just as I was the first college graduate in my family, I am also the first pentecostal. *I wailed.* I like the charismatic nefarious smashing, Bible-thumping Christians. Why? I am one of them. Be careful what you ask for. You just might get it according to God's best plan for your life: those you serve.

The Luther siblings were dedicated to God at birth and baptized as Baptists. My oldest son lives by faith. My middle son accepted the Lord at age four. My youngest son did speak in prayer language in faith similar to when I spoke "Abba" when some Pentecostal women prayed for us. I have observed he has the ability to relate on the spiritual level when he plays drums, second to none in my view, of course.

I consequently studied and applied my life to prayer. I remember the anointing would fall upon me the moment I opened the door to the restaurant where I worked. I prayed in tongues in a slightly audible, on the breath fashion, for eight hours a day; while I cooked and baked in a restaurant near our home. It was a midnight shift. No one noticed since I was the only cook. There was one waitress and one dishwasher. The owner bused. I had tremendous, alert energy to fill the orders. The window was very full again and again. We lived near the railroad yards where workers arrived and departed at all hours of the day and night.

I prayed at home loud and long. I prayed. I prayed. I prayed. God was able to answer every prayer I prayed for them abundantly. In other words, God's will on Earth is when we do our part due to intercessory prayer. He hears. He answers. *Prayer never fails, nor is anyone who prays a failure.* (Man's Search for Meaning, Arlene A. Luther) Amen!

Overcoming the Spirit of Infirmity
CHAPTER FOUR

"Then flew one of the seraphims unto me, having a live coal in his hand, which he had taken with the tongs from off the altar: And he laid it upon my mouth, and said, Lo, this hath touched thy lips; and thine iniquity is taken away, and thy sin purged"
(Isaiah 6:6, 7)

Childhood Silence

As a child I was quiet. I did not speak much, if at all. This reminds me according to Daniel's life in Daniel chapter 15: he also became dumb. Following his muteness, he became healed. According to Daniel, his lips were touched by an angel (Daniel 16). When this happened, he opened his mouth and told his story. It happens today. Further, he said he saw sorrows and lost his strength. This has happened to me so many times. I have seen and known sorrow. He was saved again in verse 18. He became strong once again. So were my lips touched with a live coal as Isaiah tells us happened to him (Isaiah 6: 6-8). This implies to me we must testify according to the healing we have received. We must declare what God has done! God saves us from the influence of fallen angels. Like Daniel, at one time I could not speak. Like Daniel, I have been healed of many problems. I was at one time seen and not heard. I now declare my story of healing and salvation.

The Lord filled in the missing piece to my silent story when I learned penicillin side effects can cause inability to speak. That is what happened to me. I finally had the missing piece I needed to write my testimony. I now know the culprit that caused my silence. I learned there are persons living in government houses from penicillin overdose. Everyone just thought I was odd or retarded or something. As I grew, I often felt awkward in social situations. My mother always told me I was above average; it is a good thing I believed her! I had the courage to keep going though everyone seemed to be far ahead of me for some reason. I was given penicillin often as a child; it was the drug of choice in those days. I know I had numerous sore throats. After many years, I had an allergic reaction to the dangerous drug. My arms began to swell. When my arms swelled to several times their normal size, a shot was administered to stop the allergic reaction. In many ways I feel better as an older woman than I ever did in school. What a difference God has made in my life. The astonishing part of this story to me as I write is how God, Jehovah-Shamah, was present with me so often when I was completely unaware of his care.

A Battle for Life

The spirit of infirmity made a further attempt to overcome me as an adult when I was about fifty years of age. It was the year of 1999. The Lord and I won the battle. We overcame a broken back at the fifth lumbar, broken neck, violent spasms from head to toe due to my smashed spinal cord, twisted between two vertebrae, and a pre-cancerous infection outbreak caused from the overdose of penicillin still in my body. It had to be expelled. Mary Garrison describes the Spirit of Infirmity in her book, How to Try a Spirit, in Luke 13:10-16 as illness, frailness, weakness, oppression in diseases, viral infections, anything that breaks down the immunity system, arthritis, and health problems.

First, the fifth lumbar slipped and twisted my spinal cord to the point of paralysis. A precancerous infection broke out all over my face and upper body. That was the zombie look to say the least of it. A broken back at the fifth lumbar and broken neck caused trauma to my physical body. I became weak. I could not breathe. My potassium level was dangerously low. An ambulance was called as I silently asked Jesus to save me. Just as I prayed, an ambulance attendant placed an oxygen mask over my nose and mouth. Jesus saves.

The Lord revealed to me as I recovered from all of this, it was the casting off, not only of the excess penicillin build up in my body, but of the external influence of a generational spirit as well. Many people in my family died at an early age from some sickness or the other. Notice there is a "physical" intrusion from the "outside" in this case of the infirm spirit. In this case it was penicillin and a broken back and neck. Clogged arteries from harmful foods or a ruined liver or lungs from smoking are other examples. Influences from outside the body to the body cause sickness. Every weakness you have means the infirm spirit is happy with his ability to passively harm you without much notice.

This is nefarious influence. Spirit of infirmity is a strong physical attack to the body to weaken or overcome the saint, often undiscerned by anyone for years. I am over it all. This is glory to God. This is the reason God is patient. God heals. God teaches. God loves. To God, it is a war to "save" humans from the influences of fallen angels that perpetually hinder us from happiness. Believe me when I tell you I am happy to be both walking and talking—literally. Praise God. Nefarious influences are the chains that have to be broken. Selah.

It is the inner spirit connection to God that overcomes such attacks in the first place. Is that not what faith is? Let me assure you, with Christ, healing is absolute in both release of healing to the vessel and the kicking off of familiar spirits we call binding the influences. The more I observe, the more I believe it is external activity from the second heaven purposed only to destroy the saint. Infirmity is often generational. The saint can pray. Thus Christ arises in victory.

Praise the Lord as we continue this glorious testimony. The following is such a nice lesson about how our ministering angels care for us through the Father's Will, Jesus, and the Holy Spirit.

Ministering Angels: Seeing in Two Dimensions to the Good

God can sometimes take you from the physical world into the spiritual dimension to point out how things happen there. God has taken me several times this way. I hope you enjoy the "seer" experiences I and the Lord had together. I have not had many. So far my "seer" experiences have been for healing and instruction. I hope to go further in healing ministry with the Holy Spirit and breakthrough further with third Heaven healing on Earth. If you "see" the knee of your guardian angel, that is not physical, but spiritual in dimension. That is what God did during this time I was barely alive.

During this battle, I oozed between two worlds. I do not want to minimize how much a spinal cord injury sets anyone back in life. If you remember Christopher Reeves, superman, you remember the severed spinal cord he died from, and the awareness he brought to such injuries. My spinal cord was not severed. It was twisted to the point of paralysis between two vertebrae. A chiropractor released me from paralysis. I believe angels ministered with him during this release.

At work again, the Lord allowed me to see the knees of my guardian angels several months after this. Their robes were white satin. I believe they were eight or nine feet tall because their knees were quite a bit higher than the cubical I worked from. The Lord taught me His compassion during this time. I feel angels were sent to watch and minister to me by Christ. It was an assignment. I was surprised. I had not asked the Lord for angels at that time. I suppose I could have died. I now ask the Lord for ministering angels every day for myself and my family.

The taller angel was standing still by my cubical. The other was pacing the aisle in front of my cubical. The amazing part of this story is how much I learned about the ministry of angels during this time. I could read and understand God's direction for my healing while I worked. Unable to lift five pounds, I was barely out of the hospital and in a mental blur. With perpetual breakouts of precancerous infection, visible scabs everywhere on my delicate skin and severe spasms every few moments from my head to my toes, I was seeing the knees of my guardian angels. God is good.

To me, that cubical was a car payment. I actually had to cheat on the test to get hired. Influenced by an angel, the man administering the test actually told me the answers after everyone left. It was my guardian angel's business to get me well and get my car paid in full. Sometimes angels come to Earth on assignment to minister to us. They also transport us. Billy Graham once said he believes it is angels that carry a spirit to Heaven.

Planned Resistance: God's Way to Healing the Physical Body

The Lord is my natural healing arsenal. He is Jehovah-Rophe, my healer. In a practical way the Lord taught me how He planned to heal my broken body. I did not have to be on prescription drugs of any kind. My M.D. prescribed vitamin B-12 injections every month. God and His angels allowed me to take power over my health problems by a planned resistance that included rest and natural supplements. You can do the same.

Anyone who has given birth naturally can endure pain. Although I never had a beating like Paul to recover from, a broken back at the fifth lumbar is the most pain physically, I had to endure. It was more painful than childbirth. I wish I could impress upon you how much a miracle it is in our present culture to endure quite a lot of pain without prescription drugs. I do not blame anyone who feels they need some help to endure severe pain. I am here to testify Jesus still does heal bodies. I learned products like COQ10 enzyme, vitamins C, E, B-12 injections, ginkgo, and essential oils like sage oil, olive oil, and lavender could heal my violent spasms.

Natural Supplements Checklist

CHAPTER FIVE

"But a certain Samaritan, as he journeyed, ...saw him, he had compassion on him. And went to him, and bound up his wounds, pouring in oil and wine...." (Luke 10:33, 34)

The following natural checklist helps to make a sturdy pilgrim. It is by no means a comprehensive list. The healing of my broken physical body took quite a few years. These supplements were discovered as I read and studied natural healing.

Algae—if you do not get enough green vegetables; algae will benefit you.

Ginkgo—comes from the Ginkgo tree located in Japan and China. It provides an oriental healing solution for the brain. It worked for me.

Sea salt—It provides natural minerals.

Natural Oils—Oils are numerous. Note some oils are for topical use. Oils can be used for aroma to heal the body. I will list a few that benefited my healing process.

Lavender and Lavender Oil—can be grown easily in your garden. It can be added to your bath or used as aromatherapy for a soothing relaxation method. I put a few drops on my pillow if my nerves have been overly active any day. It helps to fall asleep.

Sage and Sage Oil—were used by the Native Americans in boosting brain power. It is excellent for memory and clarity of thinking. I have used it when a spasm gets lodged in the crown of my head. Exercise will not disperse a spasm located there. A few drops of sage oil applied to the crown, loosed the tightness of a spasm caught at the top of the spinal column.

Olive Oil—is a healing substance used in the Bible. Remember the man caught by thieves and thrown to the side of the road, beaten and wounded. The Good Samaritan used wine to clean the wound and olive oil to heal. Some Hollywood stars take a teaspoon of olive oil every day.

Vitamin E Oil—is good at helping to heal spasms. In the early days when I had to heal from violent spasms I used vitamin E oil the entire length of my spine. It absolutely helped to heal spasms. Doctors prescribe it for heart health. It is excellent applied to the thoracic spine. You may need more supplements when your body requires much healing. When you are healthy, your body requires less help. I rotate supplements. For example, I take CoQ10 Enzyme only once a year. I take Colloidal Silver occasionally when I feel I need to from a winter cold or flu germ.

B-complex—promotes energy.

CoQ10 Enzyme—is a powerful antioxidant to every cell in your body. It supports heart health. As we age CoQ10 is depleted in our bodies and needs to be replenished.

Colloidal Silver—is important in fighting off both bacterial and viral infections.

Collagen—is an important protein in body and skin health. It supports healthy skin and natural beauty. It works well with vitamin C and B spectrum vitamins.

MSM—is an organic source of natural sulfur. It is a mineral that helps to form collagen found in connective tissue and joints.

Vitamin C—is a water soluble antioxidant. It aids collagen formation. According to Linus Pauling's White paper on vitamin C and the common cold, it helps prevent colds and maintains good overall health.

Omega 3, 6 and 9—is found in fish oil, flax and borage oils. It supports a healthy cardio vascular system.

Vinegar—one teaspoon of vinegar each day (for acidity) acts as a body cleanse. There are numerous cleanses on the market for liver, kidney, circulatory and digestion cleanses.

The Impressive Lion of Judah Versus the Destroyer Angel

CHAPTER SIX

"For I know nothing by myself; yet am I not hereby justified: but He that judgeth me is the Lord" (1 Corinthians 4:4)

The following vision releases understanding as to where love dwells, supports faith and offers clarity as to how bad the devil really is to us. This vision illustrates a salvation experience. It represents dominion: how Christ saves us as the Lion of Judah today. This is a vision of assurance for pre-rapture Christians; Clearly, you will see a Satanic assignment is crushed in this two dimensional attempted rape vision! No fallen angel could carry me off into a second Heaven portal. No, I am safely on my way to third Heaven, where God dwells. I cannot be plucked out of the hand of Jesus or my Father's hand as Apostle John tells in in John chapter 10:28, 29, simple faith works for me. What is my point here? Supernatural salvation can be a creative experience beyond the once in a lifetime "born again" experience. I hope you enjoy it.

A black hole appeared slightly above me. I had no clue

the hole was alive, or that it was a destroyer fallen angel spirit waiting to attack me. Perhaps it was the old devil himself who attempted rape under the watchful eye of Jesus. Years before this at a charismatic meeting when I was still a denominational "born again" Christian, I saw a picture of this black hole. I did not know at that time black holes actually exist in physical science in outer space. I certainly did not know a person could be sucked into one of them! Science does not know much about them. They are likely portals to and from second Heaven where fallen angels travel to and from planet Earth. Everyone knows fallen angels cannot dwell in third Heaven where God dwells. Fallen angels were cast out of third Heaven with Lucifer and his pride to second Heaven, Earth, and Hell beneath the Earth. They travel on assignment just as God's angels travel, only God's angels are on a mission of mercy while second Heaven angels are thieves.

I certainly did not know many years later the same black hole would become a live vision. I saw the black hole again only it was in two dimensions this time, not just a picture. There is a parallel story here in both the physical and spiritual realm. A broken back involves many injuries to overcome because the neurological system located in one's spine is connected to every part of one's body. In this scenario, it includes a torn pericardium: the seal that surrounds and protects the physical heart, the seal of sanctification around the spiritual heart of salvation as well.

The day of this vision, the dark angel on assignment,

ripped and tore at the seal of sanctification around my spiritual heart. The black hole I am speaking about appeared as a dark energy in the spiritual dimension. I believe it was a portal to Hell or second Heaven. I believe just as God's angels can and do carry us to third Heaven, Satan's forces attempt the same thing —to carry us to Hell.

It is good to know a renewed mind is of the essence of Christ; a Christian cannot be plucked from the hand of Christ. Just as Christians pray for deliverance, it is possible at the same time for Lucifer to assign a dark angel to attack and diminish God's plan for life. This is what happened to me. Keep in mind Christ made the final decision in these matters long ago. He reversed the curse at Calvary. Our righteous walk of salvation will be proven just as Job's was proven. I saw this angel as a gate into Hell definitely on assignment. What Christ taught me that day was some wicked angels are stronger and more powerful than we are. It is only the dominion of Christ over them and our faith that causes their defeat. The dark angel was powerful enough to overcome me if it were not for the watchful eye of warrior Christ and my steadfast faith.

I had been binding evil spirits and their fruits, and had even had minor success commanding spirits in the name of Jesus. I thought that was all there was to it. I saw some Earthbound demon spirits depart in Jesus' name. I had sensed larger spirits leave in Jesus' name. Sometimes they enter a room etc. I knew it was the name of Jesus fallen angels, demons, and even Lucifer had to obey, not you or me. I am not yet Peter or Paul! Perhaps I will have to wait to meet Peter and Paul in Heaven someday to hear about their astonishing power over the devil while they lived on Earth if ever we even think about it there. However, I do know right now what a friend I have in Jesus while I live my life on this Earth. This is how it is in my experience. When in doubt while living on Earth, I cling to Jesus.

I had no idea how deadly this angel was. I believe it may have been the perverse spirit because it destroys. Suddenly it ripped and tore at my seal of salvation in the spirit realm. This experience proved to me it is not how you feel, but the renewing of your mind: what you know that saves you. The Lord brings this to mind to assure you, the spiritual is similar to the physical experience. Both can and will be healed. This is fact. You do need a strong mind grounded in the knowledge of the Bible! It is just as easy for God to heal a spiritual wound or tear to the heart's seal as it is for Him to heal a physical wound to the heart such as a torn pericardium. Jehovah-Mikkadesh is my Sanctifier, yesterday, today and forever. God is not sometimes faithful. He is always faithful.

I realized I was unequally matched to this destroyer angel. In this adventure, Christ hid himself until the moment my heart cried to Him. He swooped in like superman and saved me once again. Instantly, the impressive Lion of Judah with a mighty laugh crashed through to hold me safe, and escape the portal to Hell. Ah! What a rescue! What a day! The old Baptist adage comes to mind as I write this episode. Once saved, always saved.

This is how it is. Praise the Lord. I did not know what to think of the amazing Lion of Judah. I clung to Jesus while he laughed out loud at the pitiful devil. Did you know Jesus roars? Judah roars! I am Judah, and I am roaring now.

My faith was still there, completely unruffled. I had found Jesus as I read the Bible. I never let Him go. Remember even Paul said, "For I know nothing by myself; yet am I not hereby justified: but He that judgeth me is the Lord" (1 Corinthians 4:4). The Lord judged me favorably and defeated the spirit with ease. Once again I found myself saved through my faith and the faithfulness of Christ (Romans 12:3). Life is good.

It was over. Yes, I had been wounded, but not without the promise of further healing as a small angel fluttered by and sewed up my torn heart. Rest assured, there is healing for both the physical and spiritual body.

The "Seer" Anointing

One-way God teaches us today is through the "seer" anointing (If you are interested in the higher levels of the seer, read The Panoramic Seer by James Maloney). It means one "sees" in two dimensions. It is all about healing in ministry found in your Bible.

When I saw the knees of my guardian angels protecting me, I was in two dimensions at the same time. This was an ordinary "seer" experience. Many Christians see angels. They learn angels protect them. The second experience is somewhat extraordinary: it portays the protection of

Christ, Himself. As Christians, we know this is true. It is the very basis of our faith. It was an illustration: I was seeing salvation in two dimensions to the good.

We can identify spirit influences if we ask God for gifts of discernment. Spirits are hidden and work outside our mind's eye behind the scenes. God has to reveal this activity to us. We must "see" in two dimensions to understand what God is teaching us. I would like to point out most of the time, it is not like some television programs where there are vivid imaginations expressed in color of hellish alien Nephilim giants on Earth again. Most of the time we can discern attitudes among people. You know what I mean. Have you ever seen a brow lifted, or a scowl? How about the twitch of a mouth, an ear pull, the head drawn back with eyes cast down, or the silent treatment? Some spirits are stronger than you are. In such instances, Christ is the victor, the deliverer.

The Lion of Judah is impressive; Jehovah-Nissi is my victory.

"*Believe on the Lord Jesus Christ, and thou shalt be saved, and thy house*" (Acts 16:31). Amen.

Some years after this, I did experience healing energy on a new level. The magnetic energy I found did fill me and heal me further. It is sometimes referred to as the latter rain. It was none other than the Holy Spirit and His work on the Earth that day. It was a promise answered. Healing is a promise. I do not see why so many people want to leave that part out.

It is like saying I do not believe people speak in tongues today. That ended with the Apostles in Acts two. No one speaks in tongues today, and if they do, they are of the devil. What? We have got to let God out of the box we want to keep Him in.

The Apostles did grieve the loss of Jesus, their best friend, and wailed out loud about it speaking in tongues in Acts chapter two. What do you think wailing is? The Apostles had a great commission entrusted to them to take the gospel into the entire world. They did speak in the heavenly language. They wailed. Intercessory prayer takes more energy than a full time job. Wail to Jesus 'til the hurt subsides (Arlene A. Luther "Wail Wrap"). He will hear you. I can tell you from experience since I worked as a laborer. Believe me. Some people still pray in tongues today. Some grieve.

Paul said he spoke in tongues more than most people. I think Paul needed more healing in both his body and spirit than most people of his day. I think I did too. Believe it. Get yourself healed! Who cares what people talk about as your intellectual critics.

Not everyone speaks in tongues. Many Christian people are both saved and at the same time apostolic whether they speak in tongues or not. What about Billy Graham? Who is more gifted than He is to speak on Earth today? He is an example of an apostle who does not speak in tongues. He is a prophet who speaks to edify the church. He interprets the scripture. It is a higher office because it teaches. I was just as much apostolic when I did not speak in tongues as a born again Christian, as I am now after my healing journey during which I spoke in tongues. It is a necessary journey for some persons, not everyone. Let us not make it a social issue. I think it depends on factors God decides severally as He Wills.

The Holy Spirit is just like Jesus in substance. He is powerful to heal. What a surge of new strength to every cell I had given to me by the Holy Spirit just as promised by the angel who sewed me up after the rescue in the vision. I have seen the Holy Spirit manifest in several ways. He floats on the air, or moves above the ground like a magnetic dove. He is powerful when He does that. I still do not comprehend how I could speak and observe Him simultaneously. He is not a wimp. He carries Scripture to the ears of listeners. He heals. He carries the healing energy of Heaven just as Christ did. He speaks. When He speaks He points to Jesus. What does Jesus do? He saves. He heals. Holy Spirit is the same substance.

The Powerless Python Spirit Versus the Ordinary Woman of Faith

CHAPTER SEVEN

"...Nothing shall by any means hurt you"
(Luke 10:19)

I am not a woman generally given to visions. So what I am going to share is as much a phenomenon to me as it may seem to you. I was taken with Christ beneath the ground to the underworld in a vision. It was dense and dark. A mammoth python spirit snake from a far distance was moving rapidly toward me. I felt unafraid because I was standing there with the resurrected Jesus of Calvary, triumphant over every spirit. I sensed the snake knew he was under the authority of Jesus, just as I was. Knowing he was under submission to Christ's dominion, he still approached me in his deception of mammoth size, because clearly, it was the only tool he had. How defeated is our foe!

I remember thinking how enormous his head was as he stopped in front of me and stared directly into my eyes with unmistakable hate. I had a "knowing" or "impression" from the Lord he was suspended in time, not just for that moment, but forever in his own poison. He was totally unable to act upon his feelings. There he was paralyzed, bound in his own venomous heart, no matter how large or fierce he appeared to be, the only power he had was to slither away.

As he disappeared from view, I sensed he wanted to strike me with the flick of his tail. If only he had not been under the victory of what Jesus did for us all. Out of sight forever, I noticed a particle of light attached to every particle of dirt. The Holy Spirit caused even the dirt underground to become permeated with warm light.

There I was thinking, how saved I am as an ordinary woman of faith. There is no effort in this on my part. Could I have saved myself? Not in any way. This is not a question mark. I am not somewhat saved. I am completely saved forever. It is a period. Jesus saves!

> *"...Nothing shall by any means hurt you."*
> (Luke 10:19).

Twenty Healing Declarations
CHAPTER EIGHT

"But the fruit of the Spirit is love, joy, peace, longsuffering, gentleness, goodness, faith, meekness, and temperance" (Galatians 5:22)

These are the elements of life that overcome nefarious influences. Working with the Holy Spirit, anyone can defeat fear, muteness, a perverse spirit, jealousy including anger, pride, sadness, physical illness, or any other lack or infirmity.

These may appear to be mountains. Be assured they can be removed through faith together with the Holy Spirit. It is not necessary for someone to give a word or lay hands upon you, although certainly these may benefit the healing process. It is the Holy Spirit who heals through his expert guidance into the knowledge you need to be healed.

Keep in mind, nefarious influences or generational curses operate through ignorance. How can you be healed of something you do not know you have? Amen. Negative spirits or thoughts operate through lack, hurt, or pride. It is not some monster created for television drama. It is your thought process. That is why the Bible heals! It heals attitudes. It is a brand new paradigm, a new way of thinking about life. It is all of a sudden virtue that leads us to happiness. It is virtue that cannot be found within self without God. Be encouraged in the Lord.

The Bible places emphasis on the thought life when confronting nefarious influences. I think thoughts are definitely an important part of the battle. I do not think they are the entire battle by any means. Thoughts are not known by others. Keep in mind, hidden acts are not known by others either. Thoughts can become actions.
The Bible points out the battle for the mind. We are told to seek the Lord and we will find mercy by the prophet Isaiah. He tells us God's thoughts are not our thoughts, nor are His ways our ways. He tells us the Lord's ways are higher than our ways and His thoughts are higher than our thoughts (Isaiah 55:6, 7, 8-9). Be encouraged Paul states, "Oh wretched man that I am" (Romans 7:24). He says, "And be not conformed to this world: but be ye transformed by the renewing of your mind, that ye may prove what is good, and acceptable, and perfect will of God" (Romans 12:2).

I Declare:

"But the fruit of the Spirit is love, joy, peace, longsuffering, gentleness, goodness, faith, meekness, and temperance" (Galatians 5:22).

"For as the heavens are higher than the earth, so are my ways higher than your ways, and my thoughts higher than your thoughts" (Isaiah 55:9).

"...for I am the Lord that healeth thee" (Exodus 15:26).

"Bless the Lord O my soul: and all that is within me bless His holy name. Bless the Lord, O my soul, and forget not all His benefits: who forgives all thine iniquities; who healeth all thy diseases" (Psalm 103:1-3).

"He healeth the broken in heart, and bindeth up their wounds" (Psalm 147:3).

"...the Lord bindeth up the breach of His people, and healeth the stroke of their wound" (Isaiah 30:26).

"But unto you that fear my name shall the Son of righteousness arise with healing in His wings" (Malachi 4:2).

"And Jesus went about all Galilee, teaching and preaching the gospel of the Kingdom, and healing all manner of disease among the people" (Matthew 4:23).

"...and healed them that had need of healing" (Luke 9:11).

"For the man was above forty years old, on whom this miracle of healing was shewed" (Acts 4:22).

"How God anointed Jesus of Nazareth with the

Holy Ghost and with power: who went about doing good, and healing all that were oppressed of the devil, for God was with Him" (Acts 10:38).

"And he said unto me, my grace is sufficient for thee: for my strength is made perfect in weakness. Most gladly therefore will I rather glory in my infirmities, that the power of Christ may rest upon me.... verse 10b "...for when I am weak, then I am strong" (Second Corinthians 12:9).

"If my people, which are called by my name, shall humble themselves and pray, and seek my face, and turn from their wicked ways; then I will hear from Heaven, and will forgive their sin, and will heal their land" (Second Chronicles 7:14).

"And he showed me a pure river of water of life, clear as crystal, proceeding out of the throne of God and the Lamb....and the leaves of the tree were for the healing of the nations" (Revelation 22:1,2).

"Blessed are the pure in heart" (Matthew 5:8).

"Finally, brethren, whatsoever things are true, whatsoever things are honest, whatsoever things are just, whatsoever things are pure, whatsoever things are lovely, whatsoever things are of good rapport, if there be any virtue, if there be any praise, think on these things" (Philippians 4:8).

"Now the end of the commandment is charity out of a pure heart, and of a good conscience, and of faith unfeigned"(First Timothy 1:5).

"Holding the mystery of faith with a pure heart" (First Timothy 3:9).

"Flee also youthful lusts; but follow righteousness, faith, charity, peace, with them that call on the Lord with a pure heart" (Second Timothy 2:22).

"For the Word of God is quick and powerful, and stronger than any two edged sword, piercing even to the dividing asunder of soul and spirit, and of the joints and morrow, and is a discerner of the thoughts and intents of the heart" (Hebrews 4:12).

Epiphany: The Happy Wedding Day

CHAPTER NINE

"And they said unto him, Ask counsel, we pray thee, of God, that we may know whether our way which we go shall be prosperous. And the priest said unto them, Go in peace: before the Lord is your way wherein ye go" (Judges 18: 5, 6)

The scene is a warm, peaceful, sunny, July day. I am happily driving my car from Omaha, Nebraska, to Tulsa, Oklahoma. I have been fasting and praying for eight hours on my way to my son's wedding.

About five minutes before arriving to Tulsa city limits, I saw the largest deer I have ever seen suddenly appear on the busy highway. I do not know where it came from. I do not know in these many lanes of traffic how it arrived in front of my car.

The Lord hears me well. I was very busy praying for a happy wedding day. Before I had time to think, the Heavens opened right before my eyes! Christ had already dispensed an angel to turn the deer to its own pathway. I have seen many deer in Nebraska, but none close to the size of that deer. I could not help but wonder what the deer in Tulsa graze upon. Thankfully, both the deer and I were still in one piece thanks to the angel on the scene.

It is a good thing I depend upon the Lord because simultaneously I found myself looking up into this magnetic energy force of bright light rather than the road. Before I could put on the brakes, it was over. I went right on to the happy wedding day event. Everything was totally perfect that day. I thanked the Lord as any mother would for all He had done before this day in my son's life and for his beautiful bride. I especially thanked him for a happy wedding day.

Later, I had the opportunity to tell this story to a scientist I met at a conference. He explained it was a nanosecond of time suspension that saved me. Angels travel faster than the speed of light if they have to. I experienced a nanosecond when I saw my granddaughter's face on her return trip from the third Heaven. You will read about that next. Now I had a scientific name for this phenomenon. The prayer burden is lifted for my family. It was forty years of my life. Now I ask the Lord, "What are you able to do with the remaining years of my life on Earth?" There is more to this phase of my story. I felt the heavenly anointing fall upon me described as the latter rain. It was the same latter rain that had healed my torn heart strings earlier. I felt the Lord was exceptionally good to me that day. I love the latter rain more than I loved the lighter, former, heavenly rain. This is Heaven on Earth. For some reason, the latter rain makes me burst into tears. I am not sure of the reason. It is Heavenly.

Surprise Vision "Caught Up"
CHAPTER TEN

"...Come up hither, and I will shew thee things which must be hereafter. And immediately I was in the Spirit...." (Revelations 4:1-2)

Perhaps the biggest surprise I had was the day I was at home praying to God about garden chimes I wanted to purchase for my granddaughter. I was caught up to a small gate in Heaven. There were six small angels present smiling at me. I didn't realize until I was returned to my sofa, my granddaughter was caught up at the same time. I know this because of the nanosecond of time more it took for her return. I looked up and saw her shining face aglow as she returned to Earth. I saw a vigor for life in her face, no infirmity whatsoever! Praise God! That is a broken generational curse right there. It was as if God was telling me nothing could stop her from being everything He wanted her to be. Then she was gone from my sight. I was moved to heavenly tears, and quite honestly did not know what to think at the time. The last thing I saw that day was my guardian angel's knee, the larger angel, next to me holding garden chimes. This was God's way of telling me His promises are real from generation to generation. Every prayer I prayed was heard. It only gets better with God. Amen!

Victory
CHAPTER ELEVEN

"Whereby are given to us exceeding great and precious promises: that by these ye might be partakers of the divine nature, having escaped the corruption that is in the world through lust"

(2 Peter 1:4)

Think about cancer. It is subversive to our healthy bodies. We continue to focus on cancer until it is gone from our lives. The laborers are many in cancer research and cancer care of the body. We even have free care for children with cancer. This gives us the hope of victory someday. The subversive culture includes poverty and lack of education for the mind. It includes lust. We tend to legalize lust through numerous laws today. Spiritual cancer includes nefarious spirits controlling individuals without their knowledge of it. It is an unseen spiritual battle. This is why the Bible points out, according to Matthew 9:37, the harvest is very large; but few laborers are in this spiritual battle of the mind. This is why subversive transgression is hard to beat. It is especially confusing for smaller I.Q.s when subversive transgression is also found in great minds and leadership for political gain. It is acceptance from man rather than God, even if the transgression may be less or unobserved, rather than more and very noticed as it is in poverty. It is the confusion it brings with it. We have a "sin all the more under grace" mentality today. It is corruption. Paul asks us in Romans 6:1 *"What shall we say then? Shall we continue in sin, that grace may abound? God forbid."* He also points out in Romans 7:7...for I had not known lust, except the law had said, Thou shalt not covet. For example, think about the fact it is the law that says abortion is legal. It may be legal. It is still corrupt. In Christ we escape the corruption of our bodies and live in hope. Everyone needs hope.

Ministry on Earth: Seed Healings

The Lord, for some reason surprises me. I think it is because I am a joy to Him. I remember I was ministering one day in response to call for those needing the baptism. I noticed the lady in front of me wanted to get her language going. I asked her if she would like ministry. Yes. She did. Then Jesus and I laid hands on her together. I sensed the overwhelming joy of the Lord as He ministered. Jesus is happy! She sensed this too, as she followed me out of the room rejoicing. We talked a bit about what a joy it is to pray. Later, her husband had discontinued his heart medication and wanted someone to pray for him. The Lord had told me to lay hands on him. I felt the Lord's hand go right through his body and touch his heart. What a surprise!

Ministry on Earth: Seed Preaching

"That whosoever believeth in him should not perish, but have eternal life. For God so loved the world, that he gave his only begotten Son, that whosoever believeth in him should not perish, but have everlasting life" (John 3:15-16).

While on a Mission Outreach to New York, the Holy Spirit opened a door to preach and teach in church following the outreach. I opened my mouth and began to speak John 3:16. To my astonishment, the Holy Spirit took my words and floated them to the ears of the people, some of whom were street persons. I spoke briefly and sang while the Holy Spirit ministered. After church a lady came up to me with pencil and paper and asked for scripture. I said it was John 3:15-16, and the Romans Road found in Romans, chapters one through ten. I asked her to read the entire book of Romans. I was surprised to see all the Holy Spirit could do with such a novice. Be blessed as you read the Romans Road penned by the Apostle Paul.

The Great Commission: Romans Road for Everyone

There are a number of key scriptures in the epistle to the Romans that perfectly build, step-by-step, the pattern for a true salvation experience. I am listing the scriptures below:

"As it is written, there is none righteous, no, not one" (Romans 3:10).

"For all have sinned, and come short of the glory of God" (Romans 3:23).

"For God commandeth His love toward us, in that, while we were yet sinners, Christ died for us" (Romans 5:8).

"For the wages of sin is death; but the gift of God is eternal life through Jesus Christ our Lord" (Romans 6:23).

"If thou shalt confess with thy mouth the Lord Jesus, and shalt believe in thy heart that God hath raised Him from the dead, thou shalt be saved" (Romans 10:9).

"For whosoever shall call upon the name of the Lord shall be saved" (Romans 10:13).

Prosperity is Answered Prayer
CHAPTER TWELVE

> *"Making request, if by any means now at length I might have a prosperous journey by the will of God to come unto you. For I long to see you, that I may impart unto you some spiritual gift, to the end ye may be established"* (Romans 1:10, 11)

A brief account of the prayers God answered for me illustrates God's ability to turn love only into prosperity. My oldest son works in computer science as Senior Software Engineer. His wife works as a professional also. He and his wife have two wonderful children. The children attend a private Catholic school near their home. They are relational, happy, smart children.

My second son graduated Sigma Cum Laude as a civil engineer. He now owns his own business. He employs skilled trade workers and college graduates. He works, it seems, twenty-four seven. He is a generous person giving his time to benefit society. He recently was married. His wife is sweet and kind.

My youngest son works for his brother as Industrial Crew Manager. He is a good friend. Everyone likes him. He is a skilled drummer, not just in technique, but in his ability to connect spiritually with his audience. He and his high school sweetheart live together.

Prosperity has everything to do with attitude, and much less to do with money, although money is important. The attitude I am speaking about is to enjoy every moment of life as it is given to you. A prosperous life expresses vigor from faith. It is the ever learning, overcoming, expectant, self-motivated, and very persistent creative human experience that really gives more than it receives. It is the life that finds its reward in useful expression of the Divine. Amen!

Summary

Goodwill toward others is the opposite of poverty. God is goodwill. God is compassion. Compassion can sometimes go farther than education or even money, especially in the spiritual realm, although education is always goodwill. Goodwill is to assist in the creation of the man God meant him to be. That is what prayer is. The heart of the matter in education is to achieve oneness with self and God in spirit, soul and body as much as each person can be enabled to be happy and prosperous.

My true dignity is found in my real relationship to God, who is always good, and my love relationship in service to others.

Success is proven at each level of my relationship to God, child to adult, because to God, it is to acknowledge who He is. *The secret to my successful deliverance is love of God.* I acknowledge God. Like a child, I ask God. Then I listen and learn as I follow the leading of the Holy Spirit in my life. I know I cannot be good without God. I know He sees me through Christ. I can only be a victorious woman of God with the Holy spirit.

As we have seen from my testimony, spirits from the underworld do not express goodwill. Just like smaller spirits, some larger spirits can work together to overthrow a person of faith; if it were possible (Romans 8:35, 37). Keep in mind these are spirits. They are not human. These spirits are old. They are fallen angels, pals of the old arch angel, Lucifer. They fell with him. They know how to influence the mind and speech of mankind. They know how to suppress and deceive. They are only one third of the created angels. They are unseen in the natural. If you are interested in additional reading to victory, Randy DeMain describes battle in prayer, promises, and breakthrough to new levels of dominion you can experience in his book, "Dominion Surges".

Part Two

How Fallen Angels Work to Hinder God's Communication to us on Earth

> *"For we wrestle not against flesh and blood, but against principalities, against powers, against rulers of the darkness of this world, against spiritual wickedness in high places"* (Ephesians 6:12).

Nefarious Influences Explained as Infirmities

There are some nefarious influences we can see. I am sure the Lord has pointed out jealousy or fear to you in everyday life. You know if someone is jealous or fearful. You know if someone is a bully (haughty). You can visibly see pride without any effort. I am sure many persons are aware of influences like this at an early age. The surprising reality is many persons do not consider these fallen spirit influences as infirmities. This would be a lack of knowledge in my view.

We all agree, sickness is weakness. Fear is usually seen as weakness. However, jealousy or haughtiness can be cleverly disguised as strengths in our society, especially in leadership. The lying spirit is often disguised because it works perfectly behind the scenes as conversation about some person. Here in America it is most often behind the back conversation. The Bible says it is gossip. In our society it is often seen as strength, when in reality it is nothing more than negative reinforcement of infirmity within a group. It is pride. It is totally against God and any knowledge of the fruit of the spirit one may know. We think these things are of no consequence and easily forgiven as innocent discussion when the unseen nefarious influence is to harm. These are issues of the heart.

Jesus addressed the prideful Pharisee leaders to their faces and did not care who heard it. Some, like Nicodemus, heard him. Most religious leaders, on the other hand, crucified the man, Jesus, in jealous anger behind his back with a lying spirit. This is not easy to see. It happened in two realms with a tongue of gossip, hidden until God revealed how much too far the damage went when Jesus died at Calvary. Innocent people are still convicted today. More often than not they are outside prison walls and merely dropped from the everyday life of society.

Nefarious Influences Identified According to the Bible:

Passive Spirits

Spirit of Fear—The spirit of fear is the opposite of faith. "For therein is the righteousness of God revealed from faith to faith: as it is written, "The just shall live by faith" (Romans 1: 17). "For God hath not given us the spirit of fear; but of power, and of love, and of a sound mind" (2 Timothy 1:7). Fear can lead to bondage. Bondage can be imposed on someone through fear of an individual; or group of people. "And deliver them who through fear of death were their entire lifetime subject to bondage" (Hebrews 2:15). I like the prayer word deliver here. Faith leads us to deliverance!

Spirit of Bondage—

"And they made their lives bitter with hard bondage..." (Exodus 1:14). Bondage was imposed upon the Hebrew people.

The spirit of bondage causes passivity. It is imposed upon someone or an ethnic group such as the Hebrew people mentioned in scripture. It suppresses. Obvious bondages are drug and alcohol abuse. Penicillin was bondage for me. It is a broken chain now. Sickness is bondage. Poor people in third world countries are in bondage to poverty.

God can and does sweep you off your feet sometimes as you move along with an encounter here and there to support a truth He is revealing to you. For me, it is a testimony of prayer to wellness.

Spirit of Heaviness: Observe Negative Energy—The spirit of heaviness, similar to other negative spirits, is dark. It did not appear to me to be dense in form like the python for example. It was like a cloud pressing over an individual. It is not easily noticed. It can be like a blanket. It can quench the Holy Spirit. I believe it varies in heaviness of appearance.

To compare it with other dark spirits is only in the awareness it is a dark spirit. I have seen ground demons that appear as dark figures. They do not have wings. Those I saw were small demons running away in Jesus name. The ground demons seem to have a slight human like form with arms and legs. I did not see any faces. The similarity to the spirit of heaviness ends with the darkness. The ground spirits had form, swift and light. The spirit of heaviness was deceptive. It appeared as a light cloud, not as dark as other dark spirits. If I sense a dark spirit I still say out loud, "In Jesus' name go."

Another comparison is large dark snake spirits with form. For example, the python spirit I told you about underground. I have seen two smaller pythons above ground. One of those clamped onto a young woman's head. I saw small legs come out of the body and clamp onto her head. I did not know it was a snake until I saw the length of the body that appeared to be the tail of the snake. I reported it to a prophet who heals in the vicinity of her dwelling. It was much smaller than the one underground. The spirit of heaviness seems to press without movement and without attachment or specific form. The individual may appear to be under a great weight. The opposite of that spirit we know is praise.

For a long time, I "saw" spirits in the second dimension before Christ moved me into the realm itself through several encounters. In Christ, the opposite of fear is faith. I wanted to discern why people act the way they do, completely unaware. As a child, I observed in pure faith. That is all I did because the penicillin inhibited my speech. This is how Christ led me, just as I was: I was unaware and now I am aware. I do not lay hands on anyone unless it is ok with the Lord.

Haughtiness is "weakness" whether it is perceived by some as strength or not. It is an aggressive bully spirit. You may not be aware this spirit expresses a lack of compassion both from the individual who has the infirmity, and to others it intentionally harms. Haughty spirits are generational. They are taught, and often as strength to survive in our competitive world. It often intimidates quietly, completely unseen, and then strikes unexpectedly. It often works with jealousy. I believe all nefarious influences are from some infirmity. All Biblically named fallen spirits produce weakness. Healing is needed both for the victim and the perpetrator by noticing the negative influence as the enemy, rather than a way to compete. As far as I am concerned it is either ignorance or lack of the knowledge of truth. We cannot let the gossip of society determine how we treat other persons.

Healing is sometimes referred to as deliverance breakthrough. I think it is an issue of the heart. You can identify the spirit by the fruit according to Mary Garrison (How to Try a Spirit by Mary Garrison). For example, gossip is a fruit of the lying spirit she tells us. You can sometimes see it in the physical realm when it is really bad. You can feel the damage. You do not have to be a part of it. It can be seen in the physical, or it can be seen in two dimensions.

Notice the second level is when God takes you into the spiritual dimension to tell you something through a vision or encounter. God is usually generous in this way because charismatic Christians place encounters on a high priority list. They place priority on healing rather than evangelism for example. This is the reason God gave me encounters to testify, to prove. Jesus was able to bring the spiritual dimension to the Earth and breakthrough as a healing evangelist, a good many times in His ministry. He brought Heaven to Earth. Forgive and heal persons. Teach, pastor and preach is what Jesus did. This is the apostolic minister's goal still today.

Active Spirits Work to Overcome God

The seducing spirit, the perverse spirit, and lying spirit often work together in aggression behind the scenes in dark sentences and actions.

Seducing Spirit—The ill will of the seducing spirit (1 John 2:26-27, Mark 13:22) leads persons into lies rather than truth. It has a double tongue. It works quietly behind the scenes and speaks in dark sentences. If it is resisted, it will cause persons to fall immediately into dark, sexual multiple contacts. It will call in the lying spirit to assist. The lying spirit will assist to cover any evil action.

Perverse Spirit—The perverse spirit is strong to overcome and control the saints of God. "Whoso walketh uprightly shall be saved: but he that is perverse in his ways shall fall at once" (Proverbs 28:18). Persons influenced by these spirits are at work behind the scenes individually and also at large. More often than not, the church is right in there with the drama these two spirits cause. Everyone often seems to be oblivious. It is the intent of the heart in the end. Ask yourself if you please man rather than God. Basically catch yourself and repent.

Lying Spirit—The lying spirit tries to cause anxiety for the Christian. It is vicious. It is one of the most aggressive spirits I have ever seen. I never noticed a spirit body. It remains hidden in human gossip. Dr. Phil in his book Life Code talks about fifteen characteristics you may observe in nefarious persons. Two of the character traits he mentions you can observe in nefarious personalities are lying and gossip. I mention these two characteristics because the Bible points these out to us. His advice is to stay away from persons like that. Good advice.

You can purchase his book by visiting his website or Amazon.com. You will need to type Dr. Phil/nefarious influences into your search engine. You will find all fifteen of them there. If the seducing spirit and perverse spirit cannot overcome an individual, the lying spirit will lie to cover the hidden corruption. It will puff up a person or group of persons in this way. It will reinforce a group usually through this type of negative unity. On the other hand, if the seducing spirit and the perverse spirit together cannot overcome an individual, the lying spirit will be added to slander the person it seeks to destroy. Often in our society today, especially in politics, we accept this on a daily basis. No wonder ordinary persons feel free to hurt others in this fashion.

The sad truth is the lying spirit tries to be omnipresent like the Holy Spirit through gossip. It is pathetic. There are most likely numerous lying spirits similar to spirits of confusion, only much larger in size. It is the spirit of gossip. This spirit uses human tongues of many individuals, often in groups bound together through soul ties to pervert God's will and action on Earth. It is the exact opposite of the Holy Spirit who reveals Truth, strength and love. It is the exact opposite of the Pentecostal prayer language. It is the best tactic the adversary could devise to mimic the Holy Spirit. There is nothing that spreads ill will faster than this spirit. These spirits are sneaky. They set traps of little spirits, spirits of confusion and harassing spirits that are mean and nasty, calculating and manipulating. They are both aggressive and unseen in the physical except for their fruit. Watch out for these because they can attract larger spirits like jealousy, fear, or lying spirits.

Spirits of Confusion—The first group of small spirits is "spirits of confusion." The spirits of confusion work in discussion groups. The spirits I saw were small fast moving spirits with keen ears and the ability to drop thoughts and twist the direction of conversation quickly before anyone had time to consider what was said. These spirits pick up on a controversial word or expression, and use it to slay "open conversation" into politically correct "silence." Only knowledge of Spirit and Truth can keep balance in a scenario like this.

I like freedom of speech that is either formal or informal conversation. Informal is apart from Robert's rules, or panel discussions. There is not too much sanctioning of speech in political debates in this country. Although the media and church groups seem to favor political correctness. I am simply saying, there are spirits of confusion at work in politics and churches. Sometimes it is fun as an American citizen to sort it all out during an election. By the way, there is too much theology in my view. We can still say what we want to for the most part. We can talk, write, and vote as we wish.

Harassing Spirits—The second nasty group of spirits the Lord showed me is "harassing spirits." These spirits I saw after I had been praying for someone. They again are aggressive. They left the person they were tormenting; but stopped near me to show me how fierce and yet subtle they were before disappearing into the dark. They were like barking dogs, but their tones were high pitched in the spirit. These spirits are undiscerned in the physical realm. Most people are not aware of the spirits causing various arguments or personal anxiety. Here again is a good time to point out the value of prayer. Prayer is superior to medications. Medications do not get rid of harmful spirits. Prayer does.

Sickness—The influence of spirits causes weaknesses in humans. What was once called evil spirits of malady and sickness in the Bible is infirmity on planet Earth today. Understand that, and you have discernment. The most obvious weakness is sickness. I remember prayer for the sick was always first at Bible study. Someone was always in the hospital for some malady. I do not think anyone really thought I was sick. I certainly did not know I was not as well as other persons who had more energy and strength. It is not acceptable to be sick. Notice how you feel. Intelligent men and women work to overcome weakness. That is all it is. If you see someone is sick or physically weak, or mentally weak, you know most likely it is linked to generational infirmity. It can be overcome. Some ER rooms have even raised the dead. So have a few apostles.

Poverty Hinders God as a Communicator

Find your poverty. Poverties: intellectual or physical, spiritual, economic class, and emotional, deny a human being of his full rightful dignity in God. Honor is for everyone in God. I honor you. You honor me. We are all on this Earth doing as much as we can to make the world a better place to live in. Why judge further? We have to have the scales removed from our eyes to see and understand our own poverty. Often it is excessive judgment. God judges. Let us allow Him to judge. Humans are not very good at it. Everyone reading this has infirmity he may be blind to understanding or covering with pride. If you are anything like me, you have to seek until you understand the Divine solution for your life. You must have something you can find to improve your life even if you are on top of it all. Your personal healing is available. I believe you will find it. Amen.

FOR FURTHER READING

The Book of Enoch

The Biblical history about the Nephilim can be researched in a book written by Randy DeMain titled "Nephilim Agenda."

"Dominion Surges" by Randy DeMain

"Spontaneous Emergence through Inquisition" by John Dewy

"Life Code" by Dr. Phil. In this book he gives advice on how to avoid persons found with nefarious characteristics such as lies and gossip

"How to Try a Spirit by the Fruits" by Mary Garrison

"Panoramic Seer" by James Maloney

What Do Friends and Colleagues Say?

Arlene A. Luther

Arlene Luther is a lady of good character. Arlene is a good manager in the handling of her finances. She does "much with little."
Tobias Pederson, Pastor 1982

Arlene's personality lends itself to a service provider field. She is fortunate to possess an even temper, compassionate disposition, and capability to relate to all ages.
Rosemary Elsberg, Friend

Arlene is a talented person, and has musical ability. In my contact with her, I have observed she works well with children.
Rev. Donald Jones, Pastor 1985

Arlene is receptive to suggestions. She puts much energy into her planning and instruction. She uses a wide variety of activities to motivate students.
Barbara Lucas, Special Projects 1986

Arlene consistently demonstrates a high level of dependability, arrives on time, and works very well with other team members. Arlene is also one of the most trustworthy employees I have had the pleasure to work

with during our time together. She has brought a lot to the team in interaction, presence, and new ideas to overcome obstacles or maintain productive and positive work.
Mandy McGinnis, Colleague, Business Manager 2002

You are truly a wonderfully remarkable woman of God, talented, beyond measure.
Blessings Sis, Deb Hayes, Colleague I.O.M. 2013

Arlene is outspoken and courageous in her beliefs.
Kris Fries I.O.M. 2013

Arlene is very detail-oriented and ambitious. She has a big heart behind her work.
Angelia Heim, Colleague, Coordinator of Volunteers and Human Resources 2014

I can tell you were spiritually motivated for the right words and melodies in your music. I finished playing through your music this morning. You have the spiritual gift of creating pleasing and singable songs. I bet each song has a story behind it. Thanks for sharing your talents with us. I feel honored to know you and sing your praises. These songs could be made into some kind of format like a Christian musical. I can tell you poured your soul, heart and passion for the creation of these songs. I liked all your songs. I will pray you will be given more melodies and words for your next adventure in song. God Bless,
Gary Koelling, Friend, Retired Music Teacher 2015

Hi, Arlene! I read through your testimony yesterday afternoon. It was so fascinating and moving! Thank-you for sharing it with us!
Cathy Koelling, Friend 2015

Spirit song of Christmas

Arlene Luther

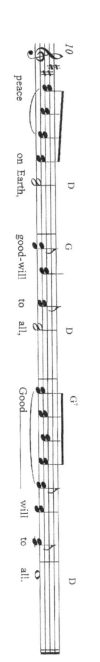
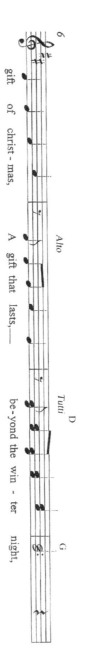
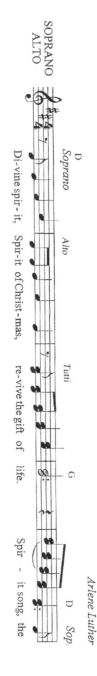

Wail Wrap

DANCE OF ZION
(HANUKKAH SEASON)

Words and Music by
ARLENE A. LUTHER

Hanukkah

May God be with us
Our Lord will pros-per us
Bless and for-give us
In Him we put our trust

Heal and pro-tect us.
That is our fu-ture

Gifts are His good-ness
Our Lord will pros-per us
Our quest will seek and
In Him we put our trust. Pros -

© 2010 ARLENE A. LUTHER
All Rights Reserved

Contact information for author:
Arlene A. Luther
4541 N. 65th St.
Omaha, NE 68104
402-547-8705

arlenealuther@gmail.com

https://www.positivepage.us/
https://hilltoprecords.com/songwriters/arlenealuther
www.youtube.com/watch?v=PnLixitAqQ

Google: "A Christmas Greeting" by Arlene A. Luther

Appendix
Songs
"Good News Fast Tract", originally published by Xulon Press

GOOD NEWS FAST TRACT

COMPLETE NEW TESTAMENT

ARLENE A. LUTHER